HEINEMANN
STATE STUDIES

Uniquely
West
Virginia

Patrick Cribben

Heinemann Library
Chicago, Illinois

© 2004 Heinemann Library
a division of Reed Elsevier Inc.
Chicago, Illinois

Customer Service 888-454-2279

Visit our website at www.heinemannlibrary.com

Designed by Heinemann Library
Printed in China by WKT Company Limited.

08 07 06 05 04
10 9 8 7 6 5 4 3 2 1

**Library of Congress
Cataloging-in-Publication Data**
Cribben, Patrick.
  Uniquely West Virginia / Patrick Cribben.
    p. cm. -- (Heinemann state studies)
  Includes index.
  ISBN 1-4034-4665-2 (lib. bdg.) --
ISBN 1-4034-4734-9 (pbk.)

  1. West Virginia--Juvenile literature. I. Title.
II. Series.

  F241.3.C75 2004
  975.4--dc22

                                    2004002779

Cover Pictures

Top (left to right) The Greenbrier, Wheeling
Suspension Bridge, West Virginia state flag,
Harper's Ferry **Main** New River Gorge
National Park

Acknowledgments
Development and photo research by BOOK
BUILDERS LLC

The author and publishers are grateful to the
following for permission to reproduce copyrighted
material:

Cover photographs by (top, L–R): Photo by
Courtesy The Greenbrier; Andre Jenny/Alamy;
Joe Sohm/Alamy; Joe Sohm/Alamy; (main):
Nowitz.com.

Title page (L–R): Photo by Phil Berry/Mountain
Berry Photos; David Fattaleh/WV Division of
Tourism; David Fattaleh/WV Division of Tourism;
p. 5, 8, 17, 21B, 26, 29, 30T, 33, 42, 44 David
Fattaleh; p. 6 Nowitz.com; p. 7, 42, 45 IMA for
BOOK BUILDERS LLC; p. 10 Steve Shaluta;
p. 11T, 18 Joe Sohm/Alamy; p. 11B One Mile
Up; p. 12 Troy & Mary Parlee/Alamy; p. 13T
Arco/J. de Cuveland/Alamy; p. 13M, 14B John &
Karen Hollingsworth/USFWS; p. 13B Eric
Engbretson/ USFWS; p. 14T Matt Wicker/Alamy;
p. 15T Glen Smart/USFWS; p. 15M Jack Dykinga;
p.15B Courtesy Barry Sutton/www.lakeneosho.org;
p. 20, 22B, 35 Culver Pictures; p. 21T AP Photo/
Library of Congress; p. 22T Hulton Archive; p. 23
AP Photo/Charles Rex Arbogast; p. 24 Courtesy
The Greenbrier; p. 25 Lynn Swann; p. 28 AP
Photo/Herald Dispatch; p. 30B Melanie Kipp;
p. 31 Renee Comet Photography, Inc./Stockfood
America; p. 32 B. Minton/Heinemann Library;
p. 36 Rick Haye; p. 37 All-Pro Photography by
Dale Sparks; p. 38 Jim Pickerell/Alamy; p. 40 Phil
Berry/Mountain Berry Photos; p. 43T Andre
Jenny/Alamy; p. 43B Courtesy Tug Valley
Chamber of Commerce.

Special thanks to Suzy McGinley of the West
Virginia Library Commission for her expert
comments in the preparation of this book.

Every effort has been made to contact copyright
holders of any material reproduced in this book.
Any omissions will be rectified in subsequent
printings if notice is given to the publisher.

Some words are shown in bold, **like this.**
You can find out what they mean by looking
in the glossary.

Contents

Uniquely West Virginia

Unique means one of a kind. West Virginia is unique; a one-of-a-kind state. With an average **elevation** of more than 1,500 feet above sea level, West Virginia is the most mountainous state east of the Rocky Mountains. West Virginia is also known as one of the nation's leading producers of coal. All but two of the state's 55 counties have coal deposits.

Origin of the State's Name

West Virginia is the only state that was created out of another state. When Virginia voted to **secede** from the **Union** in 1861 and join the **Confederacy,** people in Virginia's westernmost counties disagreed with the decision and formed their own government. In 1861, before the **Civil War** (1861–1865), all of what is now West Virginia was part of the state of Virginia. In 1863, the U.S. Congress passed a bill establishing the new state of West Virginia. President Abraham Lincoln signed the bill in 1863, making West Virginia the 35th state.

Major Cities

Charleston is the capital of West Virginia and its largest city, with a population of more than 53,000 people. The State Museum in the city's Cultural Center features exhibits that describe the history of West Virginia. The museum's exhibits include everything from a unique collection of antique hats to the telescope that George Washington used to survey the area in the 1700s.

The Capitol building is the city's most impressive architectural feature. At 293 feet high, the building's gold plated dome is the highest capital dome in the country—5 feet higher than the dome on the U.S. Capitol building in Washington, D.C.

Huntington is located at the western edge of the state near the Kentucky and Ohio borders. Incorporated in 1871, the city sprang to life as a major transportation hub for both railroads and steamboats along the Ohio River. The city is home to the Huntington Museum of Art. In addition to fine paintings and sculptures from around the world, the museum also contains a large collection of Appalachian folk art. The Museum of Radio and Technology, the largest museum of its kind in the United States, is also in Huntington. This museum features hundreds of radios from as long ago as the 1920s.

Huntington is West Virginia's second largest city with more than 51,000 residents.

Wheeling, the state's fourth largest city with a population of 31,000, is located in the far north. The city was founded in 1770. It prospered during the 1800s due to its importance as a port city on the Ohio River.

Wheeling is home to Oglebay Park, which is one of the largest and most visited city parks in the country. Oglebay's 1,500 acres include three golf courses, a museum, and its very own zoo. Each winter, the park hosts the Winter Festival of Lights, also known as "America's Largest Light Show," with more than 750,000 lights covering trees and buildings over an area of more than 300 acres.

West Virginia's Geography and Climate

West Virginia is bordered by Maryland, Pennsylvania, Ohio, Kentucky, and Virginia. Hills and mountains cover most of West Virginia. These mountains shape West Virginia's land and climate.

Located in the southern part of the state, the New River is one of the oldest rivers in the United States.

LAND

West Virginia has two major geographical regions: The Appalachian Ridge and Valley Region and the Appalachian Plateau Region. A steep ridge of mountains called the Allegheny Front runs diagonally from the northeast corner of the state to the southwest corner and separates these two regions. A small portion of the eastern panhandle of West Virginia lies in the Blue Ridge Mountain region.

The Appalachian Ridge and Valley Region, which covers about one-sixth of the state runs from the Allegheny Front eastward to the Virginia border. Here, the dense, rugged mountains dominate, with heavily forested hills separated by narrow valleys. The rich limestone soil in this region supports much of the state's agriculture and livestock.

The Appalachian Plateau region covers approximately 80 percent of the state. It includes the Kanawha plateau, which features lower elevations and deep V-shaped river valleys separated by steep-sided upland areas. Most of the state's large deposits of coal, petroleum, salt, and natural gas can be found here, along with most of its larger cities.

CLIMATE

West Virginia has a **humid continental** climate like many of the eastern states. But temperatures at higher elevations are often colder than those at lower elevations. While the average high temperature in low-lying Charleston (600 feet above sea level) in July is 87°F, the average high temperature in Elkins (1,930 feet above sea level) only 100 miles away in the eastern mountains is 83°F. In January, the temperature averages about 35°F in Charleston but only 30°F in Elkins.

Average Annual Precipitation West Virginia

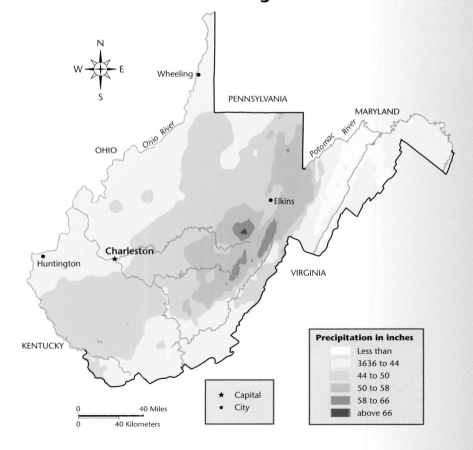

The mountainous Appalachian Ridge and Valley Region receives the most precipitation in the state.

Precipitation in inches	
	Less than 36
	36 to 44
	44 to 50
	50 to 58
	58 to 66
	above 66

★ Capital
• City

0   40 Miles
0   40 Kilometers

Famous Firsts

TRANSPORTATION FIRSTS

The first successful launch of a steamboat took place near Shepherdstown in 1787. Inventor James Rumsey loaded the steamboat with three tons of coal and several women passengers to prove that his invention could safely haul both freight and people. The boat's engine heated river water to make the steam that turned the large paddle-wheel and pushed the boat through the water.

At 3,030 feet in length, the New River Gorge Bridge in Fayette County is the longest single-span steel arch bridge in the world. The bridge rises 876 feet above the river, making it also the second highest bridge in the United States. Cables that support the bridge span 3,500 feet between two 330-foot tall towers built on either side of the river. Each year, on the third Saturday in October, the bridge is

Construction of the New River Gorge Bridge was completed in 1977 at a total cost of $37 million.

open to pedestrians, and some thrill seekers are permitted to parachute and bungee jump off of its deck.

The Huntington Electric Light and Street Railway Company opened the first commercially operated electric railroad, or "streetcar," in the world in 1892. It ran between Huntington and Guyandotte, a distance of approximately three miles.

Summers Street in Charleston was the first brick street in the world. In 1870, Dr. John Hale of Charleston developed especially hard bricks for the road. Workers laid those brick over a layer of tar-covered boards and two layers of sand. The brick road replaced a dirt road.

Memorial Tunnel, near Charleston, was the first tunnel in the country to be monitored by television cameras to improve safety. The tunnel opened in 1954 as part of the West Virginia Turnpike, but closed in 1988 when the turnpike was widened and improved. In the early 1990s, police, firefighters, and other emergency workers started using the tunnel as a training site to practice for responding to emergencies.

HISTORIC FIRSTS

The first free school for African-American children south of the **Mason-Dixon line** opened in Parkersburg in 1862. Then called the Sumner School, it taught children from grades one to twelve. In 1954, the school became the first high school in West Virginia open to both white and African-American students. Today, the original building houses an African-American history museum.

In 1928, Minnie Buckingham Harper became the first African-American woman legislator in the United States. She was appointed to the West Virginia House of Delegates to fill the unfinished term of her late husband.

West Virginia war veterans in Welch built the first memorial building to honor soldiers who fought in **World War I** (1914–1918). They dedicated the building in May 1923. Welch is also home to the first memorial to African-American veterans of World War I. It was dedicated in 1928.

FUN FIRSTS

In 1908, Anna Jarvis of Wheeling organized the first Mother's Day observance at Andrews Church in Grafton to honor her mother, who had died the previous year. She went on to organize a campaign to make Mother's Day a national holiday. President Woodrow Wilson signed a proclamation officially recognizing the holiday in 1914.

The first organized golf club in the United States was formed in 1884 at Oakhurst Links in White Sulphur Springs. The golf course still exists today. Modern golfers can play the course with the same type of equipment used in the late 1800s.

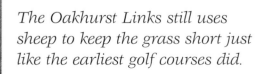

The Oakhurst Links still uses sheep to keep the grass short just like the earliest golf courses did.

West Virginia's State Symbols

WEST VIRGINIA STATE FLAG

West Virginia adopted its state flag in 1929. The two figures on the flag are a farmer, representing agriculture, and a miner, representing industry. The large rock between them symbolizes strength. The rock is inscribed with the date West Virginia joined the **Union.**

Two rifles crossed in front of the rock shows that West Virginians are prepared to fight for freedom.

WEST VIRGINIA STATE SEAL

Adopted in 1863, the seal has the same farmer, miner, and boulder as the state flag. The red "Cap of Liberty" and the state motto below it emphasize the importance of freedom to West Virginians.

STATE MOTTO: *MONTANI SEMPER LIBERI*

The state motto, *Montani Semper Liberi,* means "Mountaineers Are Always Free" in Latin. The legislature chose this motto in 1863 to emphasize the state's refusal to join the Confederacy. The act that made West Virginia a state also outlawed **slavery.**

Artist Joseph H. Diss Debar designed the state seal.

"The West Virginia Hills"

Oh, the West Virginia hills!
How majestic and how grand,
With their summits bathed in glory,
Like our Prince Immanuel's Land!
Is it any wonder then,
That my heart with rapture thrills,
As I stand once more with loved ones
On those West Virginia hills?
CHORUS:
Oh, the hills, beautiful hills,
How I love those West Virginia hills!
If o'er sea o'er land I roam,
Still I'll think of happy home,
And my friends among the West Virginia hills.

STATE NICKNAME: THE MOUNTAIN STATE

West Virginia is nick-named "The Mountain State" because mountains cover more of the state's area than in any state east of the Mississippi River.

STATE SONG: "THE WEST VIRGINIA HILLS"

West Virginia adopted its state song in 1963. Mrs. Ellen King wrote the words, and H.E. Engle wrote the music.

STATE FLOWER: RHODODENDRON

In 1903, West Virginia adopted the Rhododendron maxima, or "big laurel," as the state flower with the support of local school children. The rhododendron grows through the state.

The rhododendron is in the shrub or bush family and is recognizable by its large dark evergreen leaves and big blossoms.

STATE TREE: SUGAR MAPLE

The state legislature made the sugar maple the official state tree in 1949. Sugar maples can be found throughout the state. The wood from these trees, which grow up to 120 feet high, is excellent for furniture making.

Maple farmers also collect the sap from these trees in the early spring and boil it down to make maple syrup.

STATE BIRD: CARDINAL

The cardinal became the official state bird in 1949. Cardinals are common throughout the state.

The female cardinal has just as strong a singing voice as the male, which is unusual among birds.

STATE FISH: BROOK TROUT

The state selected the brook trout as the state fish in 1973. It thrives in the cold, spring-fed streams in the mountains and valleys of West Virginia.

A favorite fish for eating, the brook trout weighs approximately two pounds.

The original Golden Delicious apple tree was so valuable that its owners built a 30-foot high fence around it in 1914 to protect it from thieves.

STATE FRUIT: GOLDEN DELICIOUS APPLE

In 1905, Andre Mullins discovered the first Golden Delicious apple tree on his farm in Clay County. All of the Golden Delicious apple trees in the world today grew from **grafts** taken from the original tree. The Golden Delicious apple became the official state fruit in 1995.

STATE ANIMAL: BLACK BEAR

The black bear became West Virginia's official state animal in 1955. It lives primarily in the eastern mountain region of the state.

Black bears weigh up to 250 pounds and are the only species of bear found in West Virginia.

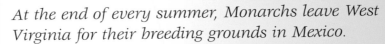

At the end of every summer, Monarchs leave West Virginia for their breeding grounds in Mexico.

STATE BUTTERFLY: MONARCH BUTTERFLY

The state legislature made the Monarch the official state butterfly in 1995. Common throughout West Virginia, this orange-yellow and black butterfly is the only butterfly that flies south for the winter like many birds.

STATE INSECT: HONEYBEE

This familiar yellow-and-black striped bee became West Virginia's official state insect in 2002. In addition to producing honey, the bee **pollinates** many of the state's fruit and vegetable crops.

STATE GEM: LITHOSTROTIONELLA

Lithostrotionella, or Mississippian fossil coral, can be found almost exclusively in the Hillsdale Limestone of Greenbrier and Pocahontas counties in the southeastern part of the state. It is not really a gemstone, but rather a type of **fossil.**

By producing honey and helping crops grow, the honeybee benefits West Virginia's economy more than any other insect in the state.

West Virginians cut and polish lithostrotionella to make jewelry and other items.

West Virginia's History & People

European settlers first crossed the Appalachian Mountains into what is now West Virginia more than 300 years ago. Long before they arrived, Native Americans had been living in the region for thousands of years.

EARLY PEOPLES

The first people to live in what is now West Virginia came to North America more than 20,000 years ago by crossing land bridges that existed between Asia and Alaska. They were **nomadic** peoples who lived in small family groups and hunted large animals.

Around 3,000 years ago, a group called the Adena people became the dominant culture in the area. These were the first Native Americans to build ceremonial mounds as part of their villages, and they are often called the Mound Builders. The mounds, which were probably built as religious or burial sites to honor Adena leaders, can still be seen in several locations in West Virginia.

Between 1000 and 1600, West Virginia was home to the Delaware, Shawnee, Susquehanna, Cherokee and several other Native American peoples. They lived in small villages where they hunted, fished, and grew corn, beans, and squash. Around 1600, the Iroquois Confederacy—an alliance that included the Mohawk, Oneida, Onondaga, Cayuga, and Seneca tribes—began to take control of the area, driving most of the other tribes from the land.

Grave Creek Mound

The Grave Creek Mound in Moundsville in Marshal County is the largest cone-shaped burial mound in the United States. It is 62 feet high, 240 feet in diameter, and contains 57,000 tons of dirt. That's more than 50 million gallon buckets of dirt. It was built between 250 and 150 B.C.E. and was a surrounded by a moat, which has since disappeared.

EARLY EXPLORERS AND SETTLERS

English colonists established the first permanent European colony in what is now the United States at Jamestown, Virginia, in 1607. Although both the British and French governments claimed much of present-day West Virginia, the mountains kept the Europeans from expanding into the territory for the next 100 years.

Englishman Morgan Morgan established the first permanent settlement in what is now West Virginia near present-day Bunker Hill in Berkeley County in 1726. By the middle of the 1700s, tensions had risen between the British, French, and Native Americans over rights to the land in the region. These disputes led to the French and Indian Wars fought between the British colonists on one side and the French and Native American tribes on the other. The wars lasted from 1754 to 1763.

Although the British had defeated the French by 1763, many Native American tribes continued to fight for the land in the area. It was not until 1774 that the Native American nations signed a peace treaty finally giving up claims to the region. The end of fighting with the Native

Americans helped allow the colonial army to focus their attention on the **Revolutionary War** with the British that started in 1775. The final battle of that war was fought at Fort Henry near Wheeling in September 1782. The signing of the Treaty of Paris the next year ended the war and gave birth to the United States.

EAST VERSUS WEST

After the Revolutionary War, more Americans began moving across the mountains into western Virginia. Many of these settlers were German, Scotch, and Irish **immigrants** who had lived in Pennsylvania and other Northern states. Most of these people lived on small farms and in small industrial towns. Frontier life in the region was difficult, and many Western Virginians were relatively poor people. Eastern Virginia, on the other hand, had many wealthy plantations and other large farms worked by African-American slaves.

After John Brown's raid in 1859, the arsenal at Harpers Ferry and the town's importance as the intersection of two major railroad lines made it an important Civil War battleground.

Throughout the first half of the 1800s, political differences developed between eastern and western Virginians, and differing ideas about **slavery** were a large part of those conflicts. Tensions came to a head in western Virginia on October 17, 1859, when an antislavery radical named John Brown raided the government weapons arsenal at Harpers Ferry. Brown led a group of 21 armed men in the attack, hoping to inspire slaves to rise up in rebellion against their owners. The raid failed, and Brown was captured, tried, and hanged. Less than two years later, the entire north and south engaged in the Civil War over slavery and other issues, during which the separate state of West Virginia emerged.

WEST VIRGINIA AND THE CIVIL WAR

Historians have often called the **Civil War** a war of brother versus brother. This may have been truer in West Virginia than in any other state. West Virginia was officially part of the southern state of Virginia during the first two years of the war. But because western Virginia shared borders and close ties with such Northern states as Pennsylvania and Ohio, the number of people supporting the **Union** and the **Confederacy** in the state was roughly equal. It was not unusual to find members of the same West Virginia family fighting on opposite sides of the conflict.

The area was the site of many significant battles during the first two years of the war. Large battles took place at Princeton, Lewisburg, Clarksburg, and Charleston. The town of Romney went back and forth between Union and Confederate control 56 times. When the Union won the battle of Droop Mountain in November 1863, it finally established its supremacy in West Virginia.

STATEHOOD

Even before the Civil War, many western Virginians had wanted to separate from the state of Virginia and form their own state. Some of them opposed slavery, like John Brown. Others felt that the elected officials from the eastern part of the state often passed laws that favored the wealthy plantation owners in the east more than the **mountaineers** in the west.

In April 1861, when Virginia voted to join the other southern states in the Confederacy and separate itself from the federal Union, many western Virginians strongly disagreed with the decision. Delegates from the western counties met in Wheeling in June to declare a separate "Virginia" government loyal to the Union. In a public **referendum** in October, the people of those counties voted overwhelmingly to form a new state. They elected delegates to a constitutional convention that met in Wheeling in November and, in February 1962, completed a constitution that would govern the new state. President Abraham Lincoln signed the law recognizing the new constitution and creating the state of West Virginia on June 20, 1863.

FAMOUS PEOPLE

Thomas Jonathan "Stonewall" Jackson (1824–1863), Confederate general. Born in Clarksburg, Thomas Jackson acquired his famous nickname at the Battle of Bull Run, which took place on July 21, 1861. When his troop lines proved unusually difficult to penetrate and a fellow general remarked, "There stands Jackson like a stone wall." He was accidentally shot by his own troops at the Battle of Chancellorsville in 1863 and died eight days later.

Booker T. Washington (1856–1915), educator. The son of slaves, Washington believed that education and economic independence were the keys to

Scholars considered "Stonewall" Jackson one of the most brilliant military leaders of all time.

social equality for African-Americans. In 1881, he founded the **Tuskegee Institute** to train African-Americans for careers in education, agriculture, and other trades. He became one of the nation's most important early champions of African-American education and civil rights.

Carter G. Woodson (1875–1950), writer/historian. Known as "the Father of Black History," Woodson was born in New Canton, Virginia, worked in the coal mines of Fayette County, and attended Douglas High School in Huntington, where he later returned as a teacher and principal. He became the second African American to earn a **Ph.D.** from Harvard University in 1913. Through his many books and magazine articles, Woodson made people more aware of the contributions of African Americans to the nation's history.

Pearl S. Buck (1892–1973), novelist. Although she was born in Hillsboro, Pearl Buck spent most of her early years in China, where her parents were **missionaries.** Her 1931 novel about the poor people of rural China, *The Good Earth*, won the Pulitzer Prize, which is a leading annual award for literature in the United States. In 1938, she became the first American woman to win the **Nobel Prize** for Literature.

Booker T. Washington was raised in Kanawha County, where he worked in the salt furnaces and coal mines as a young man.

Woodson organized the first Negro History Week in 1926. It led to the establishment of Black History Month.

Donald F. Duncan (1891–1971), inventor/businessperson. Duncan was born in Huntington. While traveling in California in 1929, he saw a Philipino man playing with a small round toy that rode up and down on a string. The man called the toy a "yo-yo," which means "come-come". Duncan changed the toy by adding a looped string that permitted the yo-yo to do tricks. Duncan's company became the world's leading maker of yo-yos.

Senator Byrd has cast more votes in the senate than any other senator in U.S. history.

Robert C. Byrd (1917–), politician. Senator Byrd was born in North Carolina but raised by his aunt and uncle in Stotesbury, West Virginia, after his mother died when he was one year old. The longest serving current member of the U.S. Senate, Byrd was first elected to the job in 1958.

Yeager's bravery and skill inspired many of the first astronauts.

Charles Elwood "Chuck" Yeager (1923–), pilot. Chuck Yeager was born in Myra. In 1947, he became the first person to travel faster than the speed of sound. Six years later, he became the first pilot to fly at twice the speed of sound.

Don Knotts (1924–), actor. Don Knotts was born in Morgantown and attended West Virginia University. Perhaps best known as Barney Fife on *The Andy Griffith Show*, Knotts also appeared in a number of TV situation comedies and movies.

John Forbes Nash (1928–), mathematician. The life of this Bluefield native was recounted in the best-selling book *A Beautiful Mind* and the popular movie of the same title. While a student at Princeton University in the 1950s, Nash helped develop the complicated mathematical theory widely known as "game theory." Later, he struggled for many years with a mental illness that interrupted his life and work. In the 1990s, he emerged from the disease and was awarded the Nobel Prize for his work in economics in 1994.

Game theory involves the mathematical study of decision-making and strategy. Professor Nash has done some of the most important and complex work in the field.

Homer Hickam Jr. (1943–), scientist and author. The son of a mining supervisor in Coalwood, Hickam started building rockets in the late 1950s with the help of his high school friends and some of the mining engineers. The teenager's rockets, which could soar five miles into the air, won first prize at the 1960 National Science Fair. After a seventeen-year career training astronauts and designing space vehicles for **NASA,** Hickman wrote about his boyhood experiences in Coalwood in the best-selling book *Rocket Boys: A Memoir*, which later became the popular movie *October Sky*.

The Greenbrier

The Greenbrier resort in White Sulphur Springs is one of the oldest and most famous resorts in the United States. Since the late 1700s, White Sulphur Springs has been host to 26 of the nation's 42 presidents, as well as many other political leaders, entertainers, and sports heroes.

HEALING SPRING WATERS

Located in the southeastern part of the state near Lewisburg, the nearby springs have attracted visitors every year since 1778 when the wife of a local plantation owner discovered that bathing in the warm, mineral-rich waters relieved her **rheumatism.** Word of the magic spring spread steadily throughout the South and up to Washington, D.C. Many of the nation's leading citizens made the long and difficult stagecoach ride there to "take the waters."

Added in the 1920s, the 250-room Greenbrier Hotel remains the resort's central architectural feature.

Wealthy southern plantation owners began building private cottages near the springs in the 1830s. By the late 1850s, several guest accommodations had also been built at the site. The largest of these was the Central Hotel, or Old White. Built in 1858, it featured the largest ballroom in the United States and a dining room that covered an area as large as three football fields. Today, guests of the Greenbrier Resort can stay either in the once-private cottages or the renovated old hotel buildings.

The Greenbrier's Famous Secret

Perhaps the most famous story of the Greenbrier involves a secret from the **Cold War.** In 1959, the Greenbrier began building a new wing. Only a few people in the U.S. Government and at the resort knew that the addition was actually just a cover story. What workers were really building was a top-secret underground bunker meant to safely house the entire U.S. Congress in the event of an attack on Washington, D.C. by the **Soviet Union.**

The two-story bunker is about the size of two football fields and has its own power plant to provide purified air underground. Government and military officials working at the site posed as television repair people to conceal their real purpose. A newspaper reporter exposed the secret in 1992, after the Cold War had ended. The government and Greenbrier opened the doors of the facility for public tours in 1995. About 30,000 tourists now visit the once super-secret bunker every year.

West Virginia's State Government

West Virginia's government is based in its capital city of Charleston. The state's constitution, or plan of government, describes how West Virginia's government is organized. The current state constitution went into effect in 1872. It is similar to the U.S. constitution that governs the nation because it divides the government into three branches: the legislative, the executive, and the judicial.

The capitol building in Charleston was designed by Cass Gilbert (1859–1934) who also designed the U.S. Supreme Court building in Washington D.C.

LEGISLATIVE BRANCH

The legislative branch makes the state's laws. As in the U.S. government, the West Virginia legislative branch consists of two groups or bodies of elected representatives, the House of Delegates and the Senate. The House of Delegates consists of 100 members who are elected by West Virginia voters every two years. The Senate has 34 members who are elected every four years. There is no limit on the number of terms a delegate or senator may serve. Any member of either group can write a bill or proposed law. A bill must be agreed to by at least half of each body of the legislature and then signed by the governor to become a law.

EXECUTIVE BRANCH

This branch of government carries out the laws passed by the legislature and signed by the governor, who is the chief executive of the state. He or she is also elected every four years. Other elected officials of the executive branch include the secretary of state, who oversees elections and state records; treasurer, who collects tax money for the state; and attorney general, who represents the state in court cases. These officials are elected for four-year terms and may serve any number of terms consecutively.

JUDICIAL BRANCH

The judicial branch interprets the laws of the state. West Virginia's judicial branch has a system of magistrate courts with 158 magistrates statewide. The number of magistrates in each county is determined by the population of the county. There are at least two magistrate

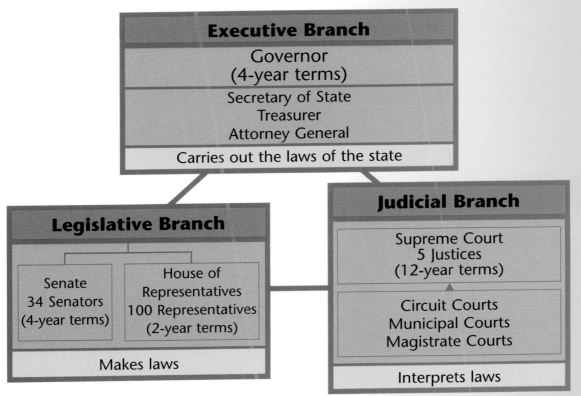

Executive Branch

Governor
(4-year terms)

Secretary of State
Treasurer
Attorney General

Carries out the laws of the state

Legislative Branch

Senate
34 Senators
(4-year terms)

House of Representatives
100 Representatives
(2-year terms)

Makes laws

Judicial Branch

Supreme Court
5 Justices
(12-year terms)

Circuit Courts
Municipal Courts
Magistrate Courts

Interprets laws

courts in every county and ten in the largest county. Magistrates issue arrest and search warrants, hear **misdemeanor criminal** cases, and hear **civil** cases with less than $5,000 in dispute.

Municipal courts established by individual towns and cities often hear cases involving such minor offenses as traffic violations. Other lower level courts include family courts that hear cases involving such matters as divorce and child custody.

The circuit courts are the major trial courts for the state. There are 31 judicial districts, or circuits, and approximately 60 judges. Each circuit serves from one to four counties. These courts hear more serious criminal cases that involve longer prison sentences, as well as civil cases involving larger amounts of money. They also hear **appeals** from the lower courts. Defendants found guilty of offenses in these courts may appeal to the supreme court of appeals, which is the highest court in the state.

The West Virginia supreme court of appeals consists of five judges who are elected by the people to any number of twelve-year terms. The longest serving member of the court becomes the **chief justice.**

Cecil Underwood: The Youngest and Oldest Governor

Republican Cecil Underwood became West Virginia's youngest governor in 1957 at the age of 34. Underwood lost elections for governor in 1964, 1968, and 1976. But he later became the oldest governor ever elected in the state by winning again in 1996.

West Virginia's Culture

West Virginia's mountain heritage has given birth to rich cultural and artistic traditions. From its wealth of folk arts and crafts, such as quilt making, basket weaving, and pottery, to its renowned mountain music and dance traditions, West Virginia has developed some of the most uniquely American means of self-expression.

FOLK ARTS AND HANDICRAFTS

Handicraft and folk festivals all over the state provide opportunities to see present-day **artisans** at work. The oldest of these is the West Virginia State Folk Festival held in the small community of Glenville each June since 1950. Craftspersons at the festival perform blacksmithing, woodcarving, weaving, and other crafts for the public. Other annual festivals include the Mountain State Folk Festival held each June in Glenville and Mountain Heritage Arts and Crafts Festival held each June and September in Charlestown.

Today, almost two-thirds of West Virginia's people still live in rural areas and small mining towns, and the long tradition of making handicrafts continues to thrive throughout the state.

THE MUSIC OF APPALACHIA

Over the years, **homesteaders** in the small mountain communities of the state have gathered together to play music, dance, and socialize. They played such traditional instruments as the fiddle, bass, guitar, banjo, and dulcimer and shared songs from their local and immigrant heritage. Many even developed ways of using ordi-

29

Skilled musicians compete for prizes honoring the best fiddle, mandolin, and bluegrass banjo players at the Vandalia Gathering.

nary household items—such as washboards, spoons, and saws—as musical instruments. The result was known as "mountain music." This is a unique blend of **bluegrass,** country, folk, and **gospel.**

A unique form of dancing also developed along with the music. In these dances, which are known as Appalachian clogging or flat-foot dances, the dancer slaps at the ground with the bottoms of his or her shoes, a little like tap dancing.

Today, many festivals held around the state preserve these unique musical and dance traditions. The Vandalia Gathering, held over four days each spring since 1975 in Charleston, brings traditional dancers together with many of the state's best known mountain musicians for concerts, contests, and demonstrations.

George Crumb

Composer George Crumb combines traditional orchestral instruments with such household instruments as toy pianos, pot lids, and saws in his musical compositions. Born in Charleston in 1929, Crumb has drawn inspiration from the mountain music he heard growing up. His pieces sometimes instruct singers to shout, hiss, or whisper. This stretches the idea of singing in ways similar to yodeling in mountain music. George Crumb won the **Pulitzer Prize** for music in 1968 for *Echoes of Time and the River.*

West Virginia's Food

The variety in West Virginia's terrain and in the backgrounds of its inhabitants make for a variety of food favorites throughout the state. In the southern and western regions, people enjoy foods similar to those found in many southern states, including fried chicken and black-eyed peas. In the northern part of the state, the immigrant traditions make Old World German and Eastern European foods such as bratwurst and goulash popular.

FOODS OF APPALACHIA

As it is in many parts of life in the Mountain State, the traditions of the mountain people are what make West Virginia cooking most unique. Rugged homesteaders had to live off the land, and their traditional sources of food and the recipes for preparing them have been handed down for generations. Hunters brought home local game for such meals as squirrel pot pie and **venison** stew. Other colorfully named traditional recipes include Seven-Day Coleslaw, Easy All-Day Stew, and Scripture Cakes, which are spice or fruit cake-like deserts made from ingredients mentioned in the Bible.

The abundance of wild berries have given the state such favorites as wild strawberry pie and rhubarb cobbler.

Colonial Cornbread

Cornbread is an easy-to-make staple of mountaineer meals. **Ask an adult to help.**

Ingredients

1 egg

1 cup milk

2 tablespoons apple cider syrup

2/3 cup cornmeal

1 cup whole corn (cooked)

3/4 cup white or whole wheat flour

1 tablespoon baking powder

1 teaspoon salt

3 tablespoons melted butter

Beat egg until light. Add milk and apple cider syrup. Mix together the egg, cornmeal, whole corn, wheat flour, salt and baking powder and gradually add to liquids. Add melted butter and cooked corn. Stir briskly. Pour into buttered 8-inch square pan. Bake at 450°F for 20 minutes.

West Virginia's Folklore and Legends

West Virginia is a state rich in legends and folktales handed down from generation to generation. Some of these stories are partly true, some are exaggerated, and some are probably almost completely made up. But all of them have helped West Virginians and other listeners understand their heritage and their community.

JOHN HENRY

Among the most famous and often-told folk stories in the United States is the legend of John Henry. It describes the life of an African-American railroad worker who pitted his hand-held hammer against a steam powered hammering machine in a contest.

John Henry was a strong and powerful man—anywhere from six feet to eight feet tall! He worked as a "gandy dancer," which meant that he pounded holes into the solid rock with a heavy hammer and spike so that other workers could drill into the holes and place explosives. This

was how companies dug holes through the mountains for railway tunnels in the early days of railroading.

When the railroad company wanted to bring in a steam drill to drill the holes, John Henry claimed that he and his hammer could get through the mountain farther and faster than the new invention. He challenged his boss and the new drill to a race through the mountain rock. With the other railroad workers cheering him on, John Henry and his heavy hammer beat the steam drill, making it through fourteen feet of rock while "the steam drill only made nine". Then, according to most versions of the tale, John Henry, exhausted by his great effort, "laid down his hammer and he died."

CORNSTALK

A certain eeriness and isolation in West Virginia's rugged mountain communities has given rise to stories of hauntings among the state's many legends and folktales. Perhaps none are more enduring than the "Curse of Cornstalk". Cornstalk was a real-life Shawnee chief who battled, then befriended, the settlers moving into his tribe's territory during the late 1700s.

Cornstalk's tribe and several others fought a great battle against American forces at Point Pleasant in 1771 near the place where the Kanawha and Ohio rivers meet. But the great chief soon made peace with his former foes. Three years later, during the **Revolutionary War,** he refused to help the British attack American forces in the area. Still, the colonial army studied his battle tactics and used them against the British in the Revolutionary War. When the chief went to the colonial fort to negotiate a peace treaty, however, the American commanders decided to hold him captive to discourage any attack by his former **allies.**

While he was held there, a group of American soldiers angry over an attack on their comrades took revenge on the Native Americans at the fort and killed Cornstalk and his son. Before he died, the great chief cursed the men who had betrayed him and the lands they had taken from his tribe.

Some people still believe that Cornstalk's curse has brought unusual misery and unexplained happenings

Like Point Pleasant, other West Virginia towns have had mining disasters. In Caples, there was an explosion in the Standard mine on August 1, 1911.

to the area. Tornados, floods, a major bridge collapse, and the worst coal mining disaster in U.S. history have all been a part of Point Pleasant's history since the death of Cornstalk.

West Virginia's Sports Teams

The mountaineer state has no major league professional sports teams. However, its college and minor league teams are a great source of pride and entertainment to thousands of sports fans. Basketball, baseball, and football are popular throughout the state, as are many other team sports.

COLLEGE TEAMS

West Virginia's colleges and universities field men's and women's teams in many different sports. The Thundering Herd of Marshall University in Huntington has many proud accomplishments. While winning the NCAA Division I-AA championship in 1996, the football team finished 15–0, becoming only the second college football team ever to win fifteen games in one season. The following year, Marshall joined Division I-A of the NCAA but kept on winning, earning five Mid-American Conference championships. Current NFL stars Randy Moss, Chad Pennington, and Byron Leftwitch all played at Marshall.

Marshall basketball star Hal Greer became the first African-American athlete in any sport to play for a West Virginia state university in 1955 and later went on to a Hall of Fame career in the

The Marshall women's tennis team won the Mid-America Conference championship three straight years from 2002 to 2004.

NBA. In addition, Marshall's women's tennis team is among the top ranked teams in the county, having won MAC Conference championships in 2002 and 2003.

West Virginia University played its first college football game in 1891. The Mountaineers went undefeated in 1988 and 1993 before losing in the national championship games in each of those years. Led by Jerry West, the Mountaineer basketball team made it all the way to the NCAA championship game in 1959 but lost a heartbreaking game, 71–70, to California.

West Virginia University shared the Big East Conference football championship with Miami University in 2003.

MINOR LEAGUE PROFESSIONAL SPORTS

From April to August, minor league baseball is popular in various parts of the state. The Bluefield Orioles and Princeton Devil Rays each play in the Appalachian League, a minor league for rookie players. Charleston has had a minor league baseball team almost every year since 1910. The current team, the Charleston Alley Cats, is affiliated with the Toronto Blue Jays and plays in the Class A South Atlantic League.

Bluefield vs. Bluefield

Bluefield, West Virginia, and Bluefield, Virginia, sit just across the border from one another, and their two high schools—Bluefield High School in West Virginia and Graham High School in Virginia—have developed a football rivalry that is rated among the top ten high school rivalries in the country. Each team plays its home games at the same stadium in Bluefield, West Virginia. Players from the two schools often have friendships, or even family relationships. During one season, the quarterback for Bluefield H.S was the son of the principal at Graham H.S.

West Virginia's Businesses and Products

Although such modern service industries as insurance, investment, and tourism have become increasingly important in the state, West Virginia's economy is still closely tied to the mineral riches found beneath its mountain soil. These natural resources include stone, salt, oil, natural gas, and, of course, coal.

MINING AND QUARRYING

Coal can be found in 53 of West Virginia's 55 counties and beneath 40 percent of its land mass. The state produced more than 175 million tons of coal in 2001 and accounts for 15 percent of all coal production in the United States. It ranks third among U.S. states in total coal production but leads the nation in underground coal production. This type of mining has a less noticeable impact on the environment than surface mining.

The type of coal found in the state is particularly valuable because it burns more cleanly than other types of coal and causes less pollution. Coal generates about 56 percent of all the electricity used in the United States and 99 percent of the electricity used in West Virginia.

By itself, West Virginia accounts for 47 percent of all coal exported from the United States to other countries.

Other products drawn from the earth in West Virginia include about 5.6 billion cubic meters of natural gas and 2.2 million barrels of crude oil each year. Salt beds in the deep mines of Marshall County produce between half a million to one million tons of salt each year. Limestone and dolomite mines and quarries in the state produce ten to thirteen tons of material each year for construction, industrial, and agricultural uses.

MANUFACTURING

Concentrated in the Ohio and Kanawha River valleys, the chemical industry is the state's leading manufacturing business. Chemical plants there, the largest of which are owned by Dow Chemical and Dupont, produce dyes, detergents, paints, plastics, and synthetic rubber. Iron and steel mills along the Ohio River in the northern panhandle are part of the state's second largest manufacturing industry—primary metals—which also includes aluminum mills in Jackson County. The leading producer of primary metals in the state is Weirton Steel, which is the state's fifth largest employer. West Virginia's third largest manufacturing sector—stone, clay, and glass products—accounts for approximately $200 million in sales each year.

TOURISM

The natural beauty of West Virginia's mountains and valleys may turn out to be the state's most precious natural resource. More than 22 million people came to West Virginia as tourists in 2001, an increase of more than four percent compared with 2000. The growing number of people coming to the state for vacations and getaways has improved West Virginia's overall economy. Tourism now employs almost twice as many West Virginians as the coal mining industry and adds about $4 billion to the state's economy each year.

Attractions and Landmarks

West Virginia features many outdoor and recreational attractions, historical landmarks, and exciting museums and other fun places to learn.

*Whitewater rafters ride in 12- to 16-foot long inflatable boats, often with a guide, or in smaller inflatable **kayaks** called duckeys.*

WHITEWATER RAFTING

Its nearly 2,000 miles of mountain streams and rivers make West Virginia the whitewater rafting capital of the world. Whitewater refers to the churning splashes of water kicked up by rapids, or especially rough spots on the river where the water pours over a drop in the rocks. This exciting outdoor adventure sport is concentrated on two rivers in the southeastern part of the state. The New River is the longest river in the world suitable for commercial rafting. The Gauley River ranks among the top five rivers in the world for whitewater adventure. There are many different levels of difficulty, or classes, of rapids. Some of them even have names, such as "Shipwreck," "Thread the Needle," and "Lost Paddle".

POINT PLEASANT BATTLEFIELD MONUMENT STATE PARK

On October 10, 1774, Point Pleasant was the site of what is often called the first battle of the **Revolutionary War.**

Virginia militiamen led by Colonel Andrew Lewis defeated several Native American tribes led by Shawnee chief Cornstalk. The defeat kept the Native Americans from forming an alliance with the British in the west. This helped the Americans win their independence. Today, an 84-foot monument stands at the spot as a reminder of the battle. The park also has a monument to the bravery of Chief Cornstalk.

ORGAN CAVE

Pioneers discovered Organ Cave, near Lewisburg, in 1704. When Thomas Jefferson visited the cave in 1791, he discovered the fossilized bones of prehistoric animals there—one of the first such finds in the country. Later exploration has proven the cave to be a major source of fossils from such extinct animals as the saber-toothed tiger and the mastodon.

During the **Civil War,** large groups of soldiers used the cave for shelter. Water that collected inside the cave was rich in potassium nitrate, which is an important ingredient in gunpowder. The cave became a major source of potassium nitrate for Confederate troops. Today, the cave features more than 40 miles of mapped passageways. Guided tours describe the cavern's many mineral deposits, including the organ-pipe shaped rock formations that give the cave its name.

SNOWSHOE MOUNTAIN RESORT

Rated as the top ski resort in the southeastern United States by *Ski Magazine* in 2003, Snowshoe's 57 downhill skiing and snowboarding slopes and trails provide the best east coast skiing south of Vermont. With its elevation of more than 4,800 above sea level and a vertical drop of 1,500 feet, the mountain offers some of the longest trails in the east. Snowboarders especially enjoy the resort's "half-pipes," which are narrow, tube-shaped slopes with high banks for performing aerial tricks and acrobatics.

Places to See in West Virginia

Wheeling Suspension Bridge
Oglebay Park
Wheeling
Moundsville Grave Creek Mound

PENNSYLVANIA

MARYLAND

Potomac River

Paw Paw
Paw Paw Tunnel

OHIO

Ohio River

Oil and Gas Museum
Parkersburg
African American History Museum

Point Pleasant Battlefield Monument State Park

Phillippi Covered Bridge
Phillippi

Snowshoe Mountain Resort
Elkins

Museum of Radio and Technology
Point Pleasant
Cornstalk Monument

National Radio Astronomy Observatory

Sunrise Museum
West Virginia State Museum
Huntington
Huntington Museum of Art
Huntington Bridge

Charleston
State Capitol Building

Green Bank

VIRGINIA

Tug Fork

FAYETTE COUNTY

Coal House
Williamson

New River Gorge Bridge

White Sulphur Springs

Lewisburg
Organ Cave

Oakhurst Links

Greenbrier Resort

KENTUCKY

★	Capital
•	City
	River
⚑	Historic Sites/Landmark
🏛	Museum
	National/State Parks, Monuments

0 ——— 40 Miles
0 ——— 40 Kilometers

Built in 1852, the Phillipi covered bridge has survived several floods and other disasters. It was carefully rebuilt using the original plans after a 1989 fire.

The lodge at the top of the mountain features seventeen different restaurants and a huge indoor swimming pool.

PHILIPPI COVERED BRIDGE

This 285-foot covered bridge is both the longest and the oldest covered bridge in the state. It is also the oldest covered bridge in the nation that is still part of a U.S. highway (U.S. 250). Nine years after its construction, the bridge became the site of the first land battle of the Civil War.

WHEELING SUSPENSION BRIDGE

At 1,010 feet long, the Wheeling **Suspension Bridge** across the Ohio River was the longest single span suspension bridge in the world when it was completed in 1849. The cost of crossing the bridge when it opened was 10 cents on a horse and $1.25 in a horse and carriage. Today, the bridge is free to travelers going between Wheeling and Bridgeport, Ohio.

In 1975, the Wheeling Suspension Bridge became the first bridge ever to be designated a National Historic Landmark.

PAW PAW TUNNEL

George Washington dreamed of linking the Potomac and Ohio Rivers by building a canal called the Chesapeake and Ohio (or C&O) canal. The most ambitious construction project on the canal was the Paw Paw Tunnel. It runs more than 3,000 feet through a rock formation called Sorell Ridge and took almost fourteen years to complete in 1850. Today, the tunnel has been drained of water and features a popular hiking and bike path. The artificial cavern is more than 25 feet high and is home to hundreds of bats.

Today, the Coal House in Williamson houses the Tug Valley Chamber of Commerce and is listed on the National Register of Historic Places.

THE COAL HOUSES

West Virginia is home to the only two buildings in the world made entirely out of coal. Built in 1933, the Coal House in Williamson on the Tug River near the Kentucky border was made from 65 tons of coal drawn from local mines during the Great Depression. Town leaders thought of the idea as a way to underscore the importance of coal in the region and the state. Builders used 30 tons of coal to build the Coal House in White Sulphur Springs, which was built as a private residence and first occupied in 1961.

SUNRISE MUSEUM

This museum near Charleston features exhibits that allow children to make pottery and tools like those used by the ancient tribes of the Kanawha valley. They can even wear clothes worn by these ancient people and see artifacts discovered in the South Charleston Mound that was built by the mound builder cultures of 2,000 years ago. The museum also features art exhibits for adults and a 65-seat planetarium in which visitors can learn about the stars in the sky.

The new Green Bank radio telescope, which opened in 2000, is the world's largest moving land-based structure.

THE NATIONAL RADIO ASTRONOMY OBSERVATORY

This modern observatory near the town of Green Bank is among the most important facilities in the world for helping scientists learn more about the universe. The site features the world's largest fully steerable telescope. Taller than the Statue of Liberty, this instrument's huge reflecting surface, or dish, which captures radio waves emitted from deep in outer space, is larger than two entire football fields. Another of the observatory's telescopes moves by rotating around a ball bearing that measures 13 feet in diameter—the largest in the world. The observatory is open to the public, and admission is free.

Map of West Virginia

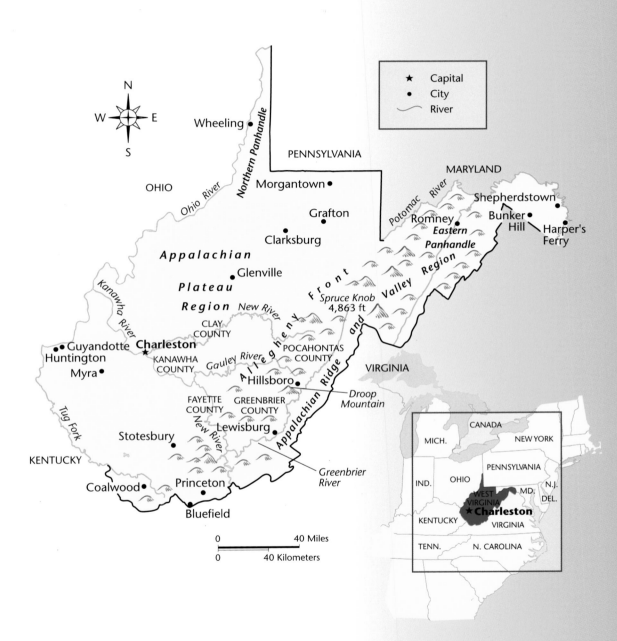

Capital ★
City •
River ∿

N W E S

Wheeling
PENNSYLVANIA
OHIO
Ohio River
Northern Panhandle
Morgantown
MARYLAND
Grafton
Potomac River
Shepherdstown
Romney
Eastern Panhandle Region
Bunker Hill
Harper's Ferry
Clarksburg
Appalachian
Plateau Region
Glenville
Kanawha River
New River
Front
Spruce Knob 4,863 ft
CLAY COUNTY
Allegheny Ridge and Valley Region
Guyandotte
Charleston
KANAWHA COUNTY
Gauley River
POCAHONTAS COUNTY
VIRGINIA
Huntington
Myra
Hillsboro
Droop Mountain
FAYETTE COUNTY
GREENBRIER COUNTY
Appalachian
Tug Fork
New River
Lewisburg
Greenbrier River
KENTUCKY
Stotesbury
Coalwood
Princeton
Bluefield

0   40 Miles
0   40 Kilometers

CANADA
MICH.
NEW YORK
IND.
OHIO
PENNSYLVANIA
N.J.
WEST VIRGINIA
MD.
DEL.
★ Charleston
KENTUCKY
VIRGINIA
TENN.
N. CAROLINA

Glossary

allies   groups or individuals associated with one another by treaty or agreement

appeal   to ask a higher court in a judicial system to review the decision of a lower court

Archaic   a variety of cultures found in North American from the period from 8000 BC -1000 BC

artisans   men or women who perform skilled work with their hands

bluegrass music   a type of county music played at a rapid tempo on banjos and guitars

ceramics   the art and process of making such products as pottery and porcelain

Chief Justice   a judge who presides over a court that has several judges, such as a supreme court

Civil War (1861–1865) in the United States, the war between the northern states loyal to the Union and the southern states loyal to the Confederacy

Cold War (1945–1990) the political conflict between the U.S. and its allies and the Soviet Union and its allies

Confederacy   the alliance of eleven southern states that seceded from the Union in 1860 and 1861 over such issues as slavery

constitution   a document that describes the fundamental political principles of a government

continental climate   a type of climate that generally features warm, humid summers and cold winters

fossil   an organic material that has been turned into a stone-like material by the passage of millions of years

frontiersmen   men and women living in unsettled or undeveloped geographical areas.

gospel music   a type of religious vocal music originating among southern African-American Christians and characterized by high emotionality

grafts   small sections of a plant used in the breeding of other similar plants

homesteaders   people who settle on land in lightly populated areas

kayaks   a small, narrow, canoe-like boat paddled by one or two riders

Mason-Dixon line   the boundary line between the Union and the Confederacy during the Civil War – states south of the line are considered to be southern states

mastodon   a large elephant-like animal with upward tusk and a hairy coat—became extinct approximately 10,000 years ago

mid-Atlantic   a region in the eastern part of the United States that generally includes the states of Delaware, Maryland, New Jersey, New York and Pennsylvania and the District of Columbia.

missionaries   people who travel to a distant place or country to teach their religion to the people who live there

mountaineers   men or women who live in a mountainous area

NASA   the National Aeronautics and Space Administration—a U.S. government agency in charge of space exploration

Nobel Prize   an award given each year to people who have achieved outstanding accomplishments in literature, physics, chemistry, or medicine

nomadic   cultures or groups that move from place to place rather than settling in a permanent site

Ph.D.   the highest degree or diploma awarded by a university in the U.S.

pollinate   to fertilize by transporting pollen from one plant to another

Pulitzer Prize   annual award given for outstanding achievements in literature, music, and journalism in the United States

referendum   a direct vote by the citizens to decide a political issue

Revolutionary War (1775–1783) a war fought between Great Britain and its colonies in North America ending in defeat for the British and the establishment of the United States of America

rheumatism   a type of arthritis or pain in the joints of the body

secede   to formally withdraw from an organization

slavery   a condition where any person or group of people is permitted to own another person or group of people as property

Tuskegee Institute   school established in 1881 to help prepare former African-American slaves for such occupations as teaching, farming, and engineering

World War II (1939–1945) international conflict fought in Europe, Asia, and Africa and involving many countries, including the U.S.

More Books to Read

Di Piazza, Domencia. *West Virginia.* Minneapolis: Lerner Publishing, 2001.

Fazio, Wende. *West Virginia.* New York: Children's Press, 2000.

Fontes, Justine and Ron. *West Virginia: The Mountain State.* New York: World Almanac, 2003.

Sommervill, Barbara A. *West Virginia (From Sea to Shining Sea).* New York: Children's Press, 2003.

Index

About the Author

Patrick Cribben is a writer and teacher who lives in neighboring Virginia. His play about coal mining towns was produced at the Greenbrier Valley Theatre near Lewisburg, West Virginia. His grandfather was a coalminer.